COSTUME

Dressing Up

Helen Whitty
POWERHOUSE MUSEUM

www.heinemann.co.uk/library
Visit our website to find out more information about **Heinemann Library** books.

To order:
 Phone 44 (0) 1865 888066
 Send a fax to 44 (0) 1865 314091
 Visit the Heinemann Bookshop at www.heinemann.co.uk/library to browse our
catalogue and order online.

First published in Great Britain in 2001 by Heinemann Library, Halley Court, Jordan Hill, Oxford
OX2 8EJ, a division of Reed Educational and Professional Publishing Ltd. Heinemann is a registered
trademark of Reed Educational & Professional Publishing Limited.

OXFORD MELBOURNE AUCKLAND JOHANNESBURG BLANTYRE
GABORONE IBADAN PORTSMOUTH NH (USA) CHICAGO

First published 2000 by
MACMILLAN EDUCATION AUSTRALIA PTY LTD
627 Chapel Street, South Yarra, Australia 3141

Cover designed by Joanna Sapwell
Interior designed by Polar Design Pty Ltd
Illustrated by Wendy Arthur
Printed in China

ISBN 0 431 14421 4 (hardback)   ISBN 0 431 14428 1 (paperback)
05 04 03 02 01   05 04 03 02 01
10 9 8 7 6 5 4 3 2 1   10 9 8 7 6 5 4 3 2 1

British Library Cataloguing in Publication Data

Whitty, Helen
  Dressing up. – (Costume)
  1. Costume
  I. Title
  391

Cover photographs reproduced with permission of Powerhouse Museum, Sydney, Australia; and
Robert Harrison (fancy dress costume).

Any words appearing in the text in bold, **like this**, are explained in the Glossary.

Contents

Don't turn this page!
Think of what you wear when you dress up. See if you recognize something you might wear in this book. There are some strange and wonderful ways of making costume!

Introduction

The things you wear on your body are your costume. You probably have things you like to wear and things you have to wear. Your family probably likes you to wear special clothes for certain occasions. Sometimes what you like to wear and what your family wants you to wear are very different. Have you heard someone say, 'I wouldn't be caught dead in that dress/jacket/hat/shoes'? People can feel very strongly about what they, and others, wear.

▼ 'FUNK INC' poster from funkessentials, designed in 1993

The story of costume is about people's creativity and the ways they like to show it. What people make, wear and care about are examples of this creativity. What people wear says something about them. *Costume* looks at wearing and making clothes across times, places and cultures.

Don't get dressed up to read this book – just dust off your imagination. Start off by imagining yourself without costume.

Too revealing? The strange thing is, the more you cover up with costume, the more you are really saying about yourself.

▶ Transparent plastic figure of a woman. It is full size, and shows the body organs, veins and arteries. It was made in 1954 to teach people about health and hygiene.

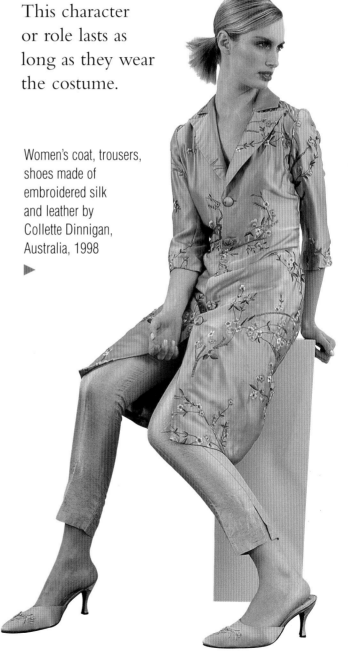

A dress made of latex (a kind of rubber).

This book is about 'dressing up'. It looks at a number of ways people dress when they are out, or part of a public display. The costumes in this book are made for decoration. In some cases, the clothes are worn by people to change themselves into another character or role. This character or role lasts as long as they wear the costume.

Women's coat, trousers, shoes made of embroidered silk and leather by Collette Dinnigan, Australia, 1998

Dressing up

…And so the Emperor marched in the procession under the beautiful canopy, and all who saw him in the street and out of the windows exclaimed: 'How marvellous the Emperor's new suit is!'
'But he has nothing on at all,' said a little child.

From *The Emperor's New Clothes* by Hans Christian Anderson, 1863

Finding yourself in a crowd of people who are all wearing clothes, and you are not, happens in a bad dream. It is also a nightmare if you are wearing clothes and they are not the right ones! We wear clothes most of the time. On certain occasions, we wear expensive or special clothes. These clothes are not worn every day but are saved for a special occasion.

What is fashion?

When many people dress up, they wear clothes that are in fashion. 'Going out' clothes are often fashionable ones. Fashion is the style of the time, or of a place or group of people. Fashion can include the shape and colour of your clothes, hairstyle and shoes, or even the way you walk and stand. Fashion can change very quickly. One year everyone is wearing cargo pants and the next year they are not. These days, fashion can vary for different ages and groups of people.

It is difficult to say when 'fashion' began. Using dress to show a person's power dates back to ancient civilizations. Kings, queens and other important people wore clothes made for them. These clothes were made of expensive cloth or were richly decorated. For hundreds of years, styles of clothing were very slow to change and could take generations. You would wear what your parents and grandparents wore when they were your age.

▶ A 'mod' girl on her Vespa scooter. She is wearing a 1967 Pierre Cardin mini-dress.

CHALLENGE 1

What costume is this from? (Hint: The costume is found in this book.)

The answer is on page 30.

Peasants wore clothes they made for themselves. Sometimes they only wore clothes allowed by law. In Europe, these laws were called **sumptuary laws** and existed up until about 1700.

In 1770, an English magazine published the first fashion 'plates', or illustrations. These helped people know what was in fashion. Before these illustrations, dolls were dressed in the latest fashion to show people what they should be wearing.

▲ A fashion plate from *Lady's Own Memorandum* book, England, 1778

▲ *The Royal Family Pop-up Book*, made of paper and cardboard, 1984. It shows the way the English Royal Family dresses for special occasions.

CHALLENGE 2

What is the fashion doll wearing in this poem called 'Lionel and Clarissa' from 1768?

Lionel and Clarissa
A coxcomb, a fop.
A dainty milk-sop;
Who, essenced and dizen'd from bottom to top.
Looks just like a doll for a milliner's shop.
A thing full of prate,
And pride and conceit;
All fashion, no weight;
Who shrugs and takes snuff,
And carries a muff,
A minikin, finiking
French powder-puff.

By Isaac Bickerstaff, 1768

The answer is on page 30.

Fashion from France

Christian Dior

Christian Dior established his fashion house in France in 1947. The Christian Dior fashion house designs and makes a small number of very expensive clothes each year for people to dress up in. France has always been famous for its fashion. Few women can afford to buy Christian Dior clothes. However, his style influences the design of less expensive clothes.

A suit and 'sack gown'

The man's three-piece suit pictured below right was made in France around 1770. The fabric is very beautiful with lines of gold thread and tiny pink and white silk rosebuds. In 1770, its wearer would probably have also worn a wig and make-up.

The woman's dress is called a 'sack gown', or *robe à la Française* (French dress). The gown is made of very expensive **brocaded** silk, which would have taken many months to weave. There is extra fabric at the back that falls from the neck to the ground.

A glamorous ivory silk-satin dress (called a 'sheath') for dressing up at night. It was designed by Christian Dior in 1957. The waist is very small and measures only ◄ 58 centimetres.

▼ A suit and 'sack gown' from France, 1770. The 'sack gown' was a very popular design for dressing up in the 1700s.

CHALLENGE ③

What does *haute couture* mean? (Hint: Christian Dior dresses are *haute couture*.)

The answer is on page 30.

Fashion from Japan

Issey Miyake

Issey Miyake, a Japanese designer, designed the lantern-shaped dress pictured right in 1995. Issey Miyake works in Tokyo and Paris, but has travelled to many parts of the world. Issey says his work is complete when the clothes are worn and moving. Things from nature, sculpture, dance, theatre, but most of all, the human form, inspire his clothes.

▲ The 'Minaret' dress made from pleated polyester by Miyake Design Studio, from a design by Issey Miyake, Japan, 1995

◀ A hand-painted silk kimono (detail pictured above) from Japan, early 1900s

The kimono

This is a kimono made in Japan in the early 1900s. It is made of dyed and painted silk. Japanese kimonos are always crossed left over right, a tradition based on Chinese fashion. Special kimonos are worn when 'going out'.

Making fabrics

Beautiful clothes to dress up in are made of beautiful fabrics. Without fabrics, there would be no clothes. Without imagination and skill, fabrics would not be beautiful or interesting. Fabrics can be made from many unusual things.

Detail from a Kuba dancing skirt. The border has been woven and embroidered with raffia-palm thread. The centre panel is made from a patchwork of bark cloth.
▼ The skirt was made in Zaire, Africa, about 1940.

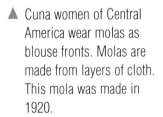 Cuna women of Central America wear molas as blouse fronts. Molas are made from layers of cloth. This mola was made in 1920.

▶ This dress is called 'Reflect', and is made by joining small pieces of Coca-Cola cans together with silver thread.

Raw materials

Fabrics can be made from plant fibres such as palm leaves, hibiscus, bark, **raffia**, cotton, **flax** or **jute**. The most common animal fibre used today is wool from sheep. Other animals have coats that can be spun into fabric – Bactrian camels, Angora rabbits, Cashmere goats and South American llamas. Fabrics can be made from minerals and metals, such as aluminium, gold and silver. Fabrics such as nylon, rayon, lycra and polyester are made using chemical processes.

▲ Detail from a contemporary raw silk **ikat** shawl

From fiber to fabric

Wool, cotton and flax are short fibres.
One long thread is made from the
short fibres in order to make cloth
by spinning. There are many ways
of turning thread into cloth, but the
most usual is weaving. For at least
9000 years, people have been weaving.
It is done on a **loom** that can be a
simple wooden frame or the latest
computer-programmed machine.

Other methods of making cloth are
felting, plaiting, knotting and looping.
Knitting and crochet are forms of
looping.

◀ A spinning wheel was once
very much a part of the home.
This spinning wheel was
made in Wales in 1760.

Adding pattern

Decoration or colour can be created in the weaving process, for example, tapestry and ikat. Decoration can also be added to fabric by painting, printing (for example, potato prints), or machine. Wax can also be used to make patterns using the resist-dying technique. Batik is an example of this.

Embroidery

Embroidery can also add pattern. Embroidery requires little in the way of tools. It is easy to set up, but takes a lot of skill.

Cutting and joining

Cutting and joining finished lengths or scraps of cloth can make beautiful patterns called patchwork and **appliqué**. This process can give new life to fabric worn in specific places.

▲ Bush tomato and flower batik design by Lena Pwerle, Australia, 1995

Adding trinkets

Bright, shining or interesting materials such as sequins, coins, beads, shells, buttons, glass and even hair can decorate fabric.

◀ Look closely at this ceremonial shirt from Cameroon, Africa. The small balls are made from human hair. The shirt was made around 1920.

CHALLENGE 4

There was a girl in our town,
Silk an' satin was her gown,
Silk an' satin, gold an' velvet,
Guess her name, three times
I've telled it.

The answer is on page 30.

Fashion from China

Stephane Dou Teng-hwang

The dress pictured right is by Stephane Dou Teng-hwang, a young dress designer from Taiwan. He designed this brightly coloured dress and others like it in 1997.

Changing styles

Style of costume in China has changed over time as it has in Europe. Look at the Chinese women's fashion timeline and compare it with the modern dress on this page. A form of costume still popular is the *cheungsam*, or *qipao*. It was first worn in the Qing dynasty (1644–1911). It was straight, loose and reached the feet. Between the 1920s and 1960s, it became very fashionable to wear when going out. People in many parts of the world copied the style. *Cheungsams* had different length hemlines, sleeves, fabrics, colours and were often very tight-fitting.

Knotted buttons and loops, known as *huaniu* or *panhuaniu*, join the collar to the **lapel**. *Huaniu* designs are often of flowers, animals and insects. Sometimes they are a sign or word that will bring good luck.

▶ Dress by Stephane Dou Teng-hwang, 1997

▲ A Chinese woman wears a *cheungsam* in this advertising poster from the 1930s.

▶ The Chinese button-knot is used on many Chinese clothes. They are comfortable to rest against and they cannot easily be broken.

Chinese women's fashion timeline, from 1100BC

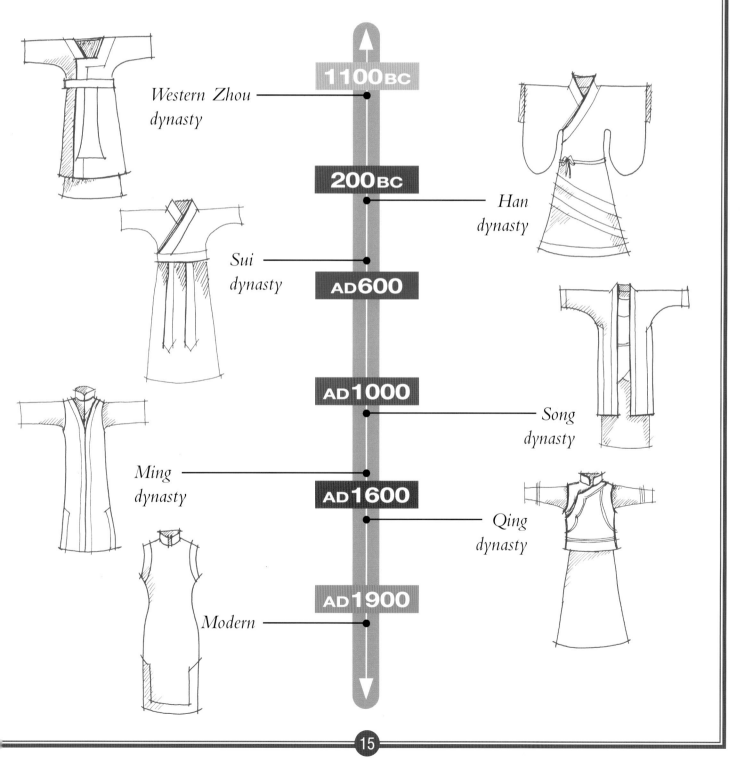

Western Zhou dynasty

1100BC

200BC

Han dynasty

Sui dynasty

AD600

AD1000

Song dynasty

Ming dynasty

AD1600

Qing dynasty

AD1900

Modern

Fancy dress

Why do people dress up as someone else? For some, it is a wish come true to be a different person, even if only for a night, like Cinderella. For others, dressing up is a chance to wear clothes that express their personality. Or it might be a chance simply to be creative.

Dressing up and wearing masks and fancy disguises have been part of festivals for centuries. Masks were used in ancient Greek and Roman theatre. Actors wore masks in plays by William Shakespeare, first performed in England in the 1500s. From the early 1700s, people wore masks to 'masquerade' – they danced, paraded in fancy dress and listened to music. Masks hid their faces and they could do things they normally would not do.

◄ This is a fancy dress costume worn by an adult to a party in 1883. The costume is of Sir Walter Raleigh (1552–1618), the adventurer and writer. Sir Walter is famous for putting his cloak over a mud puddle so that Queen Elizabeth I would not get her shoes wet and dirty.

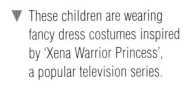
These children are wearing fancy dress costumes inspired by 'Xena Warrior Princess', a popular television series.

Both these outfits were made for children's fancy dress.

These are fancy dress costumes for children. The soldier outfit was made between 1943 and 1944, at a time when much of the world was at war. The fairy outfit was made between 1913 and 1914.

Fancy dress costumes can be based on fantasy or heroes from television or movies. Different sorts of materials, such as paper and plastic, can be used to make fancy dress. Recycled materials are often used.

Make a papier-mâché mask

What you need:

- a friend
- one handful of moisturizing cream
- 30 centimetres of clingfilm
- a paper bag
- PVA glue
- water
- water-based paint or varnish
- netball or football
- decorations, for example, glitter, feathers or beads

Step 1

Moisten your friend's face with moisturizer.

Step 2

Cover the top half of their face with clingfilm. DO NOT put it over their mouth.

Step 3

Tell your friend to keep breathing but to lie very still. Tear a paper bag into 20 strips, two centimetres wide.

Step 4

Mix $\frac{1}{8}$ cup of quick-setting PVA glue and $\frac{1}{4}$ cup of water. Run the strips of brown paper through the mixture and remove any excess with your fingers.

Step 5

Place the strips of paper over the clingfilm in different directions. Make four or five layers.

Step 6

Let the paper almost dry on your friend's face. This should only take 3–5 minutes. Your friend must lie very still – tell them stories or play their favourite music.

Step 10

Decorate the mask. You could use feathers, glitter, twigs or leaves – whatever you like!

▼ This mask is from a fancy dress outfit called 'Wood woman'. It is made of thin foam covered in wood-grain contact paper.

Step 7

Carefully lift the mask and the clingfilm from your friend's face. Then very carefully remove the clingfilm from the mask.

Step 8

Lie the mask over a netball or football to dry overnight.

Step 9

When the mask is completely dry, seal it with water-based paint or varnish.

Mardi Gras

Mardi Gras is a festival celebrated in many parts of the world. At Mardi Gras festivals, people of all ages dress up in fancy dress. Many people parade along city streets on decorated floats, in marching groups or alone in their fantasy costume. Many thousands more people watch the show.

Mardi Gras costume

Peter Tully is best known for his jewellery and costume designs. He uses objects such as throwaway toys and other cheap materials he has found. By mixing them together in unexpected ways, he changes the ordinary into the extraordinary. This is the Mardi Gras costume he made in 1990.

▶ This Mardi Gras costume by Peter Tully was made of found objects and other cheap materials.

CHALLENGE 5

On which fancy dress costume in this book can you find these shapes?

The answer is on page 30.

The idea for the 1994 Mardi Gras costume below came from a picture on a restaurant menu. Brian Ross drew an outline of himself on a wall, over which he drew the lobster. The stiffness of the costume makes it look like a toy. It is almost like a piece of Meccano.

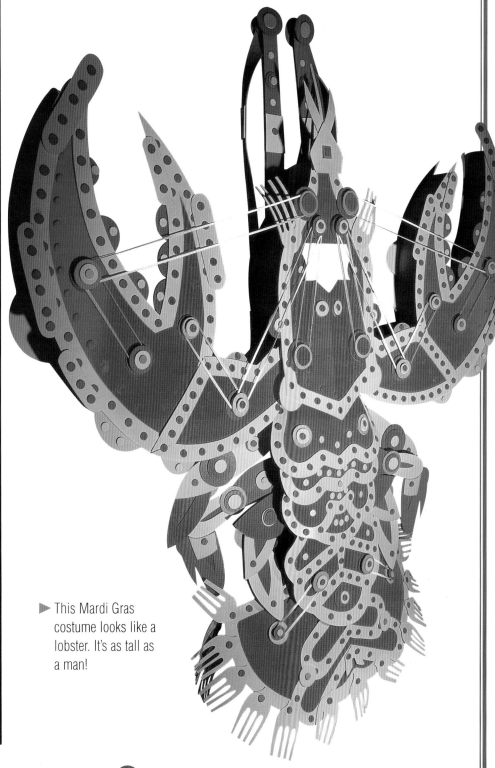

▶ This Mardi Gras costume looks like a lobster. It's as tall as a man!

Dressing up in films

Whether located in a town hall, school hall or church hall, ballroom dancing is a popular pastime. Ballroom dancers wear elaborate costumes. The film *Strictly Ballroom* is about ballroom dancing, and has many wonderful costumes. In films each actor plays a character. They dress up in the clothes their character would wear. In *Strictly Ballroom*, Scott (Paul Mercurio) is drawn into the world of flamenco, a kind of Spanish dance. In the final dance scene of the film, he wears a matador jacket with hundreds of hand-sewn sequins. His dancing partner, Fran (Tara Morice), wears a home-made flamenco dress.

▼ These sequinned and glittering costumes were made for the film *Strictly Ballroom*. The gold matador jacket alone is covered in hundreds of hand-sewn sequins.

Try this quick quiz

1 What does Xena Warrior Princess always wear on her hip?
2 In the movie *Mulan*, how does Mulan wear her hair when she pretends she is a boy?
3 What colours are the three good fairies in the Walt Disney version of *Sleeping Beauty*?

These toys were made to promote the *Star Wars* films. The toys are the same as the characters in the films. The characters created other worlds in other times. They are fantasy figures. Costumes help us to identify and recognize the characters in films. Costumes can make actors seem scary, like Darth Vader, or good, like Luke Skywalker.

What they were wearing then

Gwyneth Paltrow wore a pink satin Ralph Lauren gown with a chiffon shawl to the Academy Awards in 1999. Her hair was pulled into a classic chignon bun. Gwyneth also wore a diamond necklace and matching earrings.

4 What colour are Dorothy's shoes in the 1939 version of *The Wizard of Oz*?

5 In the television series 'Friends', which of Rachel's jobs has the most to do with clothes?

6 What does Marge in 'The Simpsons' always wear?

Meet
Stephen Curtis,
film and theatre designer

What does a designer working in film or theatre do?

They create the world that the story will happen in. They are responsible for all the things that are part of the world, such as furniture, wall colour and the costumes which people wear – everything from how to put a forest on stage to the fox's whiskers!

How did you become a designer?

When I was a child living in a country town, I enjoyed making things. One day on a Boy Scout paper drive, I picked up a Pollocks theatre and I treasured this find.

▲

Fabric swatches for 'Chook chorus' prepared by Stephen Curtis for
▼ *The Cunning Little Vixen,* 1997

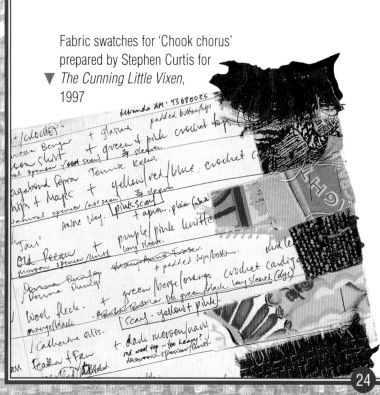

What is a Pollocks theatre?

It is a small model of a theatre made of cardboard…This little theatre had some bits missing but I was still able to put it together. The story was Aladdin. I loved it. My mother encouraged this interest and when the Melbourne Theatre Company came to our town, she arranged for me to do some workshops. I think my parents could see more clearly than I at the time that being a theatre designer was a way I could put many of my interests together.

▲ Stephen's preliminary costume drawing of 'Chook (Hen) Lady' for *The Cunning Little Vixen*, 1997

▲ Stephen's final costume drawing of 'Chook (Hen) Lady'

How long have you worked as a designer?

About 20 years in both theatre and film.

Not long ago, you designed costumes for an opera that had children in it. Tell me about your role.

The Cunning Little Vixen is the name of the opera. It is about the life of a fox caught by a hunter. In our production, children aged between 8 and 13 years played the parts of most of the forest animals. I talked with the opera's director about the messages and meanings the opera could send to the audiences. Together we decided the best way of presenting each character so the audience would understand their part in the story – the clumsy frog, the gossipy hens or the frisky vixen.

How do you design the costumes?

I do research so the costumes I design for the different characters are right for them. I like to use old photographs. For the opera, I looked at photos of animals, stuffed animals in the museum and live animals in the zoo. I made rough sketches and then final costume drawings. From here, I go shopping for materials and work with the people who make the costumes – cutters and sewers, **milliners**, bootmakers and finishers. Finishers dye fabrics and make special costume pieces. They did a really good job on the fox tails and hedgehog spines in *Vixen*.

What makes you feel good about your job?

I feel really good when an actor says that the costume I designed for them helps them find their character. Or when the audience believes in the world and characters I have created on stage or in the film.

▶ Stephen's final costume drawing of 'Fox cub number 5' for *The Cunning Little Vixen*, 1997

Clowns

The Jandaschewskys were a circus family who travelled the world performing in circuses and **vaudeville**. Performers, especially the clowns, used costumes, props and make-up to create different characters. Some of the costumes were made of pieces of other costumes. Like the performers, the costumes also had a history that could be followed.

▲ A clown suit used by the Jandaschewskys. The embroidery on this costume was taken from a much older costume and sewn onto this one. When the embroidery wore out, they added gold sequins to brighten it up.

▼ Members of the Jandaschewsky family performing as the trio Do-Re-Mi, around 1900

Rock 'n' roll stars

Elvis Presley

From the beginnings of rock 'n' roll in the mid-1950s, performers of this music set out to show that they were different from their parents. This often involved wearing hairstyles and clothes that the previous generation would not have liked. Many young people thought that Elvis Presley was the 'King of Rock 'n' Roll'. The way he looked and dressed was as much a part of his appeal as the way he performed.

▶ At the start of his career, Presley's sideburns, slicked-back hair and tight trousers were enough to set him apart from ordinary people. Once he became a big star, flashy white catsuits, like the one shown here, became his trademark.

Hush

Pop bands often wear clothes that are designed to get them noticed. Hush was an Australian band with hit singles in the 1970s. On stage they wore tight-fitting and colourful clothes and knew how to strut. Wherever they performed, crowds of weeping 'teeny boppers' would follow.

▶ A stage costume worn by Rick Lum, the bass player for Hush. It is a two-piece suit made of rayon in 1974. The words 'Get Rocked' are appliquéd onto the trouser leg. *Get Rocked* was the name of the band's latest album at the time.

Dancers

Bangarra Dance Theatre is one of Australia's most recognized indigenous dance companies. It was formed in 1989 by graduates of the Aboriginal Dance School of the Aboriginal Islander Skills Development Association. In 1996, it performed for the closing ceremony of the Olympic Games in Atlanta and in 2000 it performed at the opening ceremony of the Sydney Olympic Games. Bangarra takes its name from the Wiradjuri word meaning 'to make fire'. The Wiradjuri are an Aboriginal group in New South Wales.

Bangarra combines traditional songs and dances with modern dance to say something about Aboriginal culture today. Its costumes are modern but keep a sense of tradition. Jennifer Irwin designs most of the costumes for Bangarra. She works very closely with Stephen Page, the artistic director and choreographer, to achieve the vision he has for each production. The traditional songs and dance seen in Bangarra's work come from the Yirrkala community in Arnhem Land.

◀ A scene from 'Fish', by Bangarra Dance Theatre, 1997

Dressing up says a lot

Dressing up is about the costumes people wear in front of other people if they want to be noticed. 'Look at me,' say the costumes in this book. 'Look at how creative I am', 'Look at how beautiful I am', 'Look at, and believe in, the person I am pretending to be', 'Look and understand the real me' are some of the messages sent by the wearers of these costumes.

These costumes are works of art – from the person who made them to the person who wears them. Just as a painting, drawing, song or dance can make you feel differently about yourself or the world, so does 'dressing up'.

'Going out' clothes are not necessarily those in the latest fashion. This outfit from the Czech Republic is for wearing to church and on other special occasions. It has 18 pieces. Here it is in two stages of dress – underwear and outerwear. It is likely that three generations of women – a grandmother, mother and daughter – have worn it.

Answers

Page 7
1. The Sir Walter Raleigh costume on page 16.

2. The doll is wearing a hat.

Page 8
Haute couture means fashionable and expensive dressmaking. *Couture* is from the French word for 'sewing' and *haute* is from the French word for 'high'.

Page 13
The girl's name is Ann.

Page 20
The circles of tin are from the Xena fancy dress costume on page 17. They are cut from aluminium cake tins.

Page 22
1. Xena wears a chakram – a circular spinning blade that always finds its mark, and its way back to Xena's hands.
2. Mulan pulls her hair into a tight top-knot.
3. The three good fairies are coloured green (Flora), pink (Fauna) and blue (Merryweather).
4. Dorothy has ruby shoes.
5. Rachel is a clothing consultant for Bloomingdale's, a New York department store.
6. Marge always wears very large beads and a green dress.

Glossary

appliqué a type of embroidery where a large piece of fabric is decorated by smaller pieces of other fabrics sewn onto it

brocaded when a fabric is woven in an all-over raised pattern of flowers and/or figures in two different colours

diamantes buttons or little pieces of shiny metal or glass sewed or glued onto a costume to decorate it

felting matting together wool, fur or other fibres to make fabric

flax a plant grown for its fibres. Smooth and strong flax fibres are woven to make linen.

ikat a type of woven fabric made mostly in Indonesia

jute a strong fibre used to make rope or sacks. Jute can be mixed with silk or wool and made into fabric for clothes.

lapel the part of a coat or dress collar folded back over your chest

loom a machine for weaving cloth

milliner person who makes or sells hats

papier-mâché a strong substance made of paper pulp mixed with glue

raffia a fibre obtained from the leaves of a palm tree that is used to weave baskets or hats. Raffia thread can also be used to embroider or decorate hats or bags.

sumptuary laws laws against personal habits, including costume, that were thought to offend the wider community

vaudeville light, theatrical entertainment, mainly with musical and comedy acts

Index

Photo and object credits

All objects featured in this publication are from the Powerhouse Museum collection and all photographs are by the Powerhouse Museum, unless otherwise indicated below. Collection objects are reproduced by permission of the designers or makers listed. The museum acknowledges the many generous donations of objects, which form a significant part of its collection.

p3 'Minaret' dress by Miyake Design Studio; p4 funkessentials poster by Sara Thorn and Bruce Slorach; p5 latex dress by Steven Bruton of Tragedy, Australia, 1997; outfit by Collette Dinnigan 1998; p6 girl on Vespa from a photo by Henry Talbot, permission Neale Talbot; p8 evening dress by Christian Dior, Christian Dior Couture; p9 'Minaret' dress by Miyake Design Studio; p11 'Reflect' dress by Pearl Rasmussen Australia, 1998; p12 ikat shawl by Lise Cruickshank, Australia, 1983; p13 batik by Lena Pwerle,

Utopia Awely Batik, Northern Territory, Australia; p14 dress by Stephane Dou Teng-hwang, photo by Mai Hsin Yun; pp16/17 fancy dress costumes by Robert Harrison; p19 'Wood woman' mask by Brenton Heath-Kerr, Australia, 1993, by permission of Irene Flanagan and Brendon Williamson; p20 'Mardi Gras' by Peter Tully, Australia, 1990, permission Merlene Gibson; p21 'Lobster Mornay' by Brian Ross, Australia, 1994, permission Ross family; p22 *Strictly Ballroom* costumes by Angus Strathie for M&A Film Corporation 1992; p23 Gwyneth Paltrow photo, Austral Press Agency; p24-25 fabric plan and drawings by Stephen Curtis 1997; p27 Elvis Presley photo, Rex Features; p28 Hush costume by Rick Lum; Bangarra photo, Ashley de Prazer for Bangarra Dance Theatre 1997; p31 drawing by Stephen Curtis.

Please visit the Powerhouse Museum at **www.phm.gov.au**